The Da

The Budd...

Death and Eternal Soul in Buddhism

The Dalai Lama
The Buddha Nature

Death and Eternal Soul in Buddhism

Bluestar
Communications
Woodside, California

Translated by Christof Spitz

First published in German by Aquamarin Verlag, Germany under the title:
Die Buddha-Natur
Tod und Unsterblichkeit im Buddhismus

Copyright © 1996 by Aquamarin Verlag

This translation:

Copyright © 1997 Bluestar Communications
44 Bear Glenn
Woodside, CA 94062
Tel: 800-6-Bluestar

Revised and edited by Catherine Hunter
Cover Art by Georg Carl
Photos: Astrid Jung, Georg Carl

First printing 1997

ISBN: 1-885394-19-5

Footnotes 2, 3, 5, 6, 8,11, 12, 14, 15, 17, 18, 22, 23, 26, 27 are partly derived
from: The Shambala Dictionary of Buddhism and Zen. Translated by Michael
Kuhn, © 1991. Reprinted by arrangement with Shambala Publications, Inc., 300
Massachusetts Avenue, Boston, MA. 02115.

Library of Congress Cataloging-in-Publication Data

Bstan-'dzin-rgya-mtsho, Dalai Lama XIV, 1935-
   The Buddha nature : death and eternal soul in Buddhism / Dalai Lama.
      p. cm.
   Includes bibliographical references.
   ISBN 1-885394-19-5
   1. Buddhism--Doctrines.   2. Dge-lugs-pa (Sect)--Doctrines.
I. Title.
BQ7935.B774B83 1997
294.3'423--dc20
                                                              96-27536
                                                              CIP

Printed in Hongkong

Contents

Acknowledgment

My special thanks is offered to the secretary of His Holiness, Tsering Tashi, who not only arranged our talk, but was also extremely helpful and loving during our stay in Dharamsala.

I would also like to thank Georg Carl for his brilliant photographs, which document a piece of Tibetan history in exile. But, most of all, I am indebted to Annette Wagner who, with unbounded patience as my travel companion, helped me through intense mood swings and distress over the often incredible poverty of India, my spiritual homeland.

Regarding the American edition, I would like to thank Catherine Hunter for her excellent editorial work.

Dr. Peter Michel, Grafing, September 1996

Foreword

A wise Zen master once said, "Words are but an imperfect tool, however we don't have a better one. Therefore, we try to express spiritual things with words." At another time and place, somebody else used nearly the same words to define the shortcomings of democracy.

And how imperfect still is the world we are living in! In my view, the only meaningful way to overcome this imperfection is work. Work on ourselves and on our environment, work on the problems in our daily lives. The book you are holding in your hands is not an easy book. But it is not easy to work on yourself either.

In Tibet, for more than one and a half millennia, the wisest of the wise ones have been conducting research on the nature of the human mind—theoretically and, thanks to Buddhist meditation, in practice as well.

I don't know anyone better suited to explain the results of this work than the head of all Tibetan Buddhists, His Holiness the XIV Dalai Lama. In these days, as the time of hope for his suffering people in Tibet fades away in front of our eyes with every passing day, his message becomes more and more important.

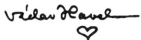

Václav Havel, Prag, October 1996

Preface

Death and immortality has been an important topic in the dialogue on the teachings of the Buddha. This topic has naturally led to questions on individuality and the continuity of life. The wide-spread idea that the *anatman* [1] teachings negate eternal individuality, has led to misunderstandings, especially among practitioners of Western religions.

During his frequent travels in Europe and the United States, His Holiness the Dalai Lama has addressed this question during talks and discussions, but never in much detail. During my first talk with him, at the Salzburg Festival in 1995, an attempt was made to tackle this question. But, due to a very busy schedule, His Holiness was forced to leave our discussions unfinished. Instead, he invited me to the north Indian town of Dharamsala, seat of the Tibetan government in exile, to continue our discussion on this topic.

Despite the availability of modern transportation, the journey to Dharamsala was still a pilgrimage. As a travel-weary European—after thirty hours on airplanes, trains and cars—I felt ashamed of my suffering after I learned about the incredible hardships the Tibetans had to endure while escaping their homeland and becoming refugees in India. I was

---

[1] This technical term, anatman (non-Self), refers to everything that is experienced as being different from the transcendental Self (atman). That is, the phenomenal world and the ego personality. Anatman in Buddhism refers to nothing has an eternal essence.

deeply touched by the Tibetan people, often humble men and women, who are distinguished by a unique love and devotion for their Dalai Lama. I will never forget an old, bent Tibetan woman who tried to enter a temple where His Holiness had recently celebrated a puja (a religious ceremony). Unfortunately, she was kept away by security guards, and was only able to make it to the entrance through endless patience. This women seemed like a symbol, an incarnation of the Tibetan destiny—complete devotion to the Buddha and the Dalai Lama, yet deeply marked by a life of suffering (see page 49).

The meeting with the Dalai Lama was blessed, for the new Tibetan Cultural Center, Norbulingka Institute, was inaugurated on the day after our arrival in Dharamsala. Built with money from His Holiness' Nobel Peace prize and the help of a Japanese sponsor, it is a unique cultural monument. In the future it will become an invaluable resource for the Tibetan Buddhist culture (see pages 50-52). One of its goals is to encourage inter-religious dialogue, and our talk with His Holiness was the first milestone in this mission.

After extensive security controls, the Dalai Lama greeted us lovingly in his reception room on the upper floor of the Norbulingka Institute's new temple. To me, who had only seen him in Europe, His Holiness appeared to be even more powerful in his own environment, where he seemed to be deeply rooted in his own energy field. One might expect to meet only a Buddhist monk, as His Holiness often describes himself, but a visitor who meets him in Dharamsala, without any doubt, encounters an incarnation of Avalokiteshvara, the Boddhisattva [2] of compassion.

Our discussion became intense very quickly. How important the topic was to His Holiness became clear when he stopped speaking in English and answered questions in Tibetan, so he could be more philosophically precise. During our discussion, time seemed to stop and only at the farewell, when the Dalai Lama offered us white scarves, did the sense of time continue to flow again.

In the forecourt of the temple the otherworldly sounds of Tibetan musicians as well as dancers greeted us and, once again, made us aware of the hard reality of India.

Dr. Peter Michel, Grafing, March 1996

---

[2] The literal translation of this Sanskrit term is 'enlightenment being.' In Mahayana Buddhism, a bodhisattva is a being who seeks Buddhahood through the systematic practice of the perfect virtues, but renounces complete entry into Nirvana until all beings have been saved. The motivation for their action is compassion, supported by highest insight and wisdom. Bodhisattvas offer active help and are ready to take the suffering of all other beings upon themselves and exchange their own positive karmic merit for the negative karma of other beings.

I.
Buddha Nature

Dr. Peter Michel: May I start with a very personal question, which is based on many statements you have made in teachings. If you look back in time, the Pali Canon[3] says, *"Monks, there is something unborn, not created, unmade."* This appears to be a statement about the Absolute in Buddhist philosophy. In your Harvard Lectures[4] you say, *"In the system of the Mind Only School Following Scripture,[5] Buddha nature is identified as a seed of uncontaminated exhaled wisdom, which is in the mind basis of all."* Then you quote from the teachings of Highest Yoga Tantra,[6] saying, *"The innermost, purest spirit, the clear light, is unborn."* In France

---

[3] The canon of the Hinayana school, which regards itself as the school closest to the original form of Buddhism. Its canon, composed in Pali, presents the views of the Theravadins, which are based directly on the teachings or words of the Buddha.

[4] H.H. the Dalai Lama, *The Dalai Lama at Harvard*, translated and edited by Jeffrey Hopkins, Snow Lion Publications: Ithaca, New York, 1988.

[5] The Mind Only, or Chittamatra, school is divided into two key factions — Followers of Scripture and Followers of Reasoning. The school's central concept is that everything that can be experienced is "mind only." Things exist only as processes of knowing, not as objects. They have no reality outside the knowing process. The external world is purely mind. Just as there are no things or objects, there is also no subject who experiences them. Perception is a process of creative imagination that produces the appearance of outer objects.

[6] Tantra means continuum or system. The tantric tradition is based on human experiential potential and describes spiritual development in terms of the categories of ground, path and fruition. The ground is the practitioner; the path is the path of meditation, which purifies this ground; and fruition is the state that arises as a result of tantric practice. All forms of tantra relate to these three phases. The Tibetan tradition speaks of four classes of tantra—action tantra, elaboration tantra, yoga tantra and highest yoga tantra. The criteria for this classification are the differences in the spiritual capacities of practitioners and the corresponding effectiveness of the means for leading them to enlightenment.

last year you said, *"Consciousness has no beginning. A consciousness can only emerge from something that is an unchanging source—that is from another consciousness—not from something lifeless. Therefore, we say that it is without beginning."* I would like to combine these statements to ask if there is a relationship between that which is unborn and unmade and the seed of Buddha nature? How does the seed come into existence? And how can the seed not be aware of its real essence?

His Holiness the 14th Dalai Lama: Regarding the explanations on Buddha nature, we must take into account the four Buddhist schools of tenets.[7] On the one hand, we have the assertions of the lower schools—the Vaibhashika and Sautrantika—and, on the other hand, the assertions of the higher schools—the Chittamatra and Madhyamika. Within the two higher schools, further distinctions can be made. The two lower schools are similar in that they focus primarily on how to observe good or ethical

---

[7] The ultimate experience of reality lies beyond words and conceptual thought. Analytical training in preparation for and during the practice of meditation is essential in attaining particular forms of direct and non-conceptual perception. A correct non-conceptual realization begins with a correct conceptual framework. As a result, the *Buddhist schools of tenets* are a means of ultimate transformation. They identify the exact nature of the misconception of phenomena and the subsequent destruction of that misconception. The four major schools of Buddhist tenets are ranked according to the subtlety with which they identify and rectify the various forms of ignorance considered to prevent liberation or omniscience. They are Vaibhasika, Sautrantika, Chittamatra and Madhyamika.

conduct. To address your questions, the two higher schools are particularly relevant.

According to the Chittamatrin, Buddha nature is the seed of an uncontaminated mind. They explain that Buddha nature is consciousness that is a conditioned, impermanent phenomenon. According to the Madhyamikas, Buddha nature refers to the emptiness or suchness of the mind, which is its ultimate nature. In particular, it refers to the suchness of a mind whose level is still in the contaminated state, one that has not eliminated the stains and hindrances. This corresponds to the teachings of the Perfection of Wisdom Sutras. Once these stains have been eliminated, that same ultimate nature of the mind is part of the Truth Body, or *Dharmakaya,* [8] of a Buddha. Since, in this school, Buddha nature is considered to be the ultimate nature of the mind, it is a permanent, unconditioned phenomenon.

According to Maitreya's *Uttaratantra,* [9] which belongs to the same school of tenets, Madhyamika

---

[8] Dharmakaya is the true nature of a Buddha or the Truth Body. It is timeless, permanent, devoid of characteristics and free from all duality. It is the body which all Buddhas have in common.

[9] A text attributed to Maitreya with a commentary by Asanga, who lived in India during the 4th century. After being inspired by the Bodhisattva Maitreya, Asanga is believed to have written five treatises in Sanskrit, after having heard them from Maitreya in the Tusita heavens. Tibetan tradition is based on a full translation of Asanga's ancient Sanskrit text. It attributes the verse section to Maitreya and the prose commentary to Asanga. The verse is considered to be Maitreya's ultimate doctrine, which is based on the Buddha's Prajnaparamita or Perfection of Wisdom sutra.

philosophy, the main purpose of using the term "Buddha nature" is to reveal the mere luminosity and cognitive nature of the mind.

In the tantric context, Buddha nature refers mainly to the clear light mind itself and not to the nature of the mind in general, namely its luminosity and cognitive faculty.

II.
The Clear Light Mind

PM: In France last year, you said clear light should not be confused with a creator or concept such as Brahman.[10] *"The tantric tradition explains the Dharmakaya through the concept of the clear light or the true nature of the mind. This means that all phenomena, samsara and nirvana manifest from this clear and shining source. Therefore, one can say that this highest source, the clear light, is close to the concept of a creator. But one should be careful. When I speak about a source, it should not be mis-understood! I do not mean that somewhere a form of concentrated clear light exists as a substrate, similar to the non-Buddhist idea of Brahma. This shining space must not be deified!"*

If this holds true, how is the clear light, which is the essence of the individual being, connected to the limited personality of this being?

DL: If you investigate, and try to find out where this clear light mind is, you will be able to find it only within an individual person. For example, we speak about human beings. They are born. This means each human being is born as an individual and has his own experience of birth. At the same time, however, we can speak of human beings collectively. The same goes for consciousness. What we identify as the clear light always belongs to an

---

[10] The impersonal Absolute beyond all distinctions.

individual—it is not Brahman or a universal soul. Since each individual's future and present experiences are based on that clear light, it is appropriate to say that the clear light acts almost like a creator. This does not mean that a separate, isolated, universal clear light exists somewhere.

PM: Can the clear light be seen as something active?

DL: No. In our normal states we cannot call clear light active. Through meditation or training, however, once we intentionally experience the manifestation of clear light, it can be used for perceiving or realizing objects. Perhaps, at that particular point, you could call the clear light mind active.

PM: Does the clear light exist as a potential in every living being?

DL: No, it is always there. You can compare it with water. When water is muddy, the purity of the water is still there. But, because the water is mixed with dirty substances, you cannot identify it. If the pure water were not there, the muddy water could not exist. The existence of the dirty water itself proves that pure water is its basis. At this moment, the clear light is inactive, but it exists. Because clear light is there, the different states of consciousness and constituent factors can arise.

PM: My main difficulty with this philosophy is understanding how the clear light can become unknown. How can a living being forget its Buddha nature, if it is always there?

DL: Our everyday consciousness is on a very gross level. When we think, "I say this, I know that," we are referring to a very gross level of consciousness. All these thoughts are on such a level. At present, the gross level of consciousness is active and the clear light level is innate. When the clear light becomes active, the gross level becomes inactive. For this reason, when we are in a deep, dreamless sleep, we are not aware of it, although we experience it. If we have a clear dream, we can remember dreaming this or that the next day. After sleeping deeply without dreaming, we wake the next morning, feeling hardly any time has passed. We sleep soundly, and after waking, look at our watch and see that several hours have passed, but it feels like just a moment. This shows that our mind has different levels.

PM: How can Buddha consciousness, which exists from the very beginning, fall into a state in which it forgets itself? For example, a Buddha was not a Buddha from the very beginning. He developed, thus there was only a seed at the beginning. Has the seed an evolutionary force in it?

DL: No. This seed has existed as long as consciousness has existed. Consciousness has no beginning. Life has no beginning.

PM: How does a person become a Buddha if there is no beginning? Do we have a wrong sense of time here?

DL: One becomes a Buddha through transformation of the mind. However, you do not have to transform the clear light mind. It is already there.

PM: We have to transform the unclear mind into the clear mind? Is that how it can be expressed? Is it like changing the dirty water to clean water? How does this happen?

DL: Through purification; by removing ignorance.

PM: That makes sense. But how did the clean water become dirty in the first place?

DL: The clear light mind becomes shrouded or unclear because of our inborn ignorance, which also exists since beginningless time. The concept of beginningless mind, or of beings living since beginningless time, cannot be proven directly, by itself. We must look at it the other way round. If you accept the beginning of living beings, then the question is how did this begin? What was the cause? The assumption of a beginning gives rise to a number of contradictions.

PM: Does the quotation from the Pali Canon at the beginning of our interview—about something unborn, uncreated and unmade—refer to the clear light mind?

DL: No. There, Buddha is teaching the non-self, or selflessness of the person (anatman), meaning the non-existence of an absolute, independent self (atman). He is referring to emptiness and not to selflessness, in the sense of not being selfish. The Pali Sutras of the Theravada [11] and the Sanskrit Sutras of the Mahayana [12] always refer to emptiness as the unborn, unabiding, unceasing. These all relate to

---

[11] A school of Hinayana Buddhism. In the ancient Pali language, Theravada means "teaching of the elders of the order." This school was founded by Moggaliputta Tissa and brought to Ceylon in 250 BC. Today the Theravada school is widespread in Southeast Asian countries, such as Sri Lanka, Burma, Thailand and Laos. As the only surviving school of Hinayana Buddhism, it regards itself as the school closest to the original form of Buddhism. The emphasis of the Thervada is on the liberation of the individual, which takes place through one's own effort in meditation and through observing the rules of moral discipline and a monastic lifestyle.

[12] A school of Buddhism literally translated from the Sanskrit as "great vehicle." The Mahayana school arose in India during the 1st century. It is called great vehicle because it opened the way of liberation to a great number of people and is based on the intention to liberate all sentient beings. Hinayana and Mahayana schools

non-self, or selflessness. In Tantra, the subtle mind of clear light is also called "unborn and uncreated." Even on the conventional level, there is good reason for doing so, as this mind is without beginning. However, this is an exception. Generally speaking, when one talks about a phenomenon that arises and ceases as being free of arising and cessation, one is referring to the ultimate mode of existence of that phenomenon, its non-self. There is no other way of interpreting this.

---

are both rooted in the teachings of the historical Buddha, but stress different aspects of those teachings. While the Hinayana school seeks liberation for the individual, the Mahayana school seeks to attain enlightenment for the welfare of all living beings. This attitude is embodied in the Mahayana ideal of the Bodhisattva, whose distinguishing quality is compassion. The Mahayana school places less emphasis on monasticism than does the Hinayana school. The lay person can also attain Nirvana and rely on the active help of Buddhas and Bodhisattvas. The Mahayana is divided into a series of schools that spread from India to Tibet, China, Korea and Japan.

III.
Self and Non-Self

PM: This brings me to the third question. In 1993, you spoke in France about the theory of self and non-self. You said that the existence of an eternal, individual, independent self is denied in Buddhism, but not the existence of an acting self, an acting power. You also said—which I found very interesting—that, after realizing Buddhahood, the individual spiritual being continues. We can, therefore, speak of the individual identity of a Buddha. How does the individual identity of a Buddha connect with the theory of the self. Is there not a parallel?

DL: No. The term "atman" has a different connotation. It refers to a self, or person, completely independent of the psychophysical aggregates. Atman is a self that can be identified apart from body and mind. This kind of self is refuted in Buddhism.

The clear light itself is not the person or a sentient being, but the basis of such a being. It is a part of consciousness and is, therefore, the basis of designation of a sentient being, of the self, or a person. But it is not the self itself. Once Buddhahood is attained, there are no longer any gross levels of thought. They have all ceased. What remains is only the clear light. At that time, the identity of the Buddha is designated by the combination of subtle mind and subtle energy. So, apart from these five subtle aggregates, there is no separate identity of a Buddha. In Buddhism there is no theory of a soul, or a self, neither on the level of ordinary beings nor on that of a Buddha.

PM: So non-self does not mean there is no individual, is that correct? The self as you interpret it is something static, as in Advaita-Vedanta.[13] You merge into Brahman, so that the atman becomes Brahman, and only Brahman exists. You disagree with that, don't you?

DL: When we refute the soul, or atman, theory, we are refuting the theory of a substantial, independent person. There is no independent self that exists substantially, from its own side. However, the self, or person, does exist dependent on the psychophysical aggregates. This applies to all beings, from the level of ordinary sentient beings up to Buddha. This self, which is designated by the psychophysical aggregates, is of course an individual, as it can only exist in relation to its aggregates. There is no all-pervasive or universal person separate from them. Anatman, or non-self, is in fact a quality, a characteristic, of each individual person. There is no universal non-self that exists separate from individual persons. Anatman is the mere negation of

[13] Advaita-vedanta literally means "the non-dual end of the Vedas" and refers to the metaphysics expounded in the Upanishads and all those scriptures that are based on the Upanishads, in one way or another. Non-dualism (advaita) is the dominant philosophical tradition within Hinduism and has many schools.

a self that is supposed to exist in such a way, substantially and independently of the psychophysical aggregates.

PM: Does the independent self dissolve itself? In Advaita-Vedanta the self ceases to exist. Atman becomes Brahman and in the end there is only Brahman.

DL: No, this is not what is meant. We are not talking about the end of something, or a process in which the self gradually dissolves. Non-self is simply a natural aspect of the way in which every person exists.

IV.
Buddhahood

PM: During a teaching in Bodhgaya, you said: "*But the basic, ultimate, innermost subtle consciousness will always remain. It has no beginning, and it will have no end. That consciousness will remain. When we reach Buddhahood, that consciousness becomes enlightened all-knowing. Still, the consciousness will remain an individual thing. For example, the Buddha Shakyamuni's[14] consciousness and the Buddha Kashyapa's[15] consciousness are distinct individual things. This individuality of consciousness is not lost upon the attainment of Buddhahood.*" Does that mean that the evolution of consciousness never comes to an end? Is there a cosmic Buddha?

DL: There is no such cosmic consciousness into which you merge.

PM: I only suggested that as an analogy for endless spiritual progress. In a statement on enlightenment, Krishnamurti[16] explained, "*Believe me,*

---

[14] The historical Buddha belonged to the Shakya clan. He received his epithet after he had separated himself from his teachers and resolved to find the way to enlightenment. The name of Shayamuni is often used in association with Buddha to distinguish the historical Buddha from other Buddhas.

[15] The Buddha of the world age preceding the present one.

[16] Jiddu Krishnamurti was born in 1895 as a poor Indian boy. He was 'discovered' by Charles W. Leadbeater, one of the spiritual leaders of the Theosophical Society at that time, and declared the vehicle of the coming World Teacher. In 1929, Krishnamurti disassociated himself from the Theosophical Society and became one of the most revolutionary philosophers of modern times. For more information see: Peter Michel, *Krishnamurti—Love and Freedom*, Bluestar: Woodside, 1995.

I only see a fragment of the infinite.... It is not possible to be one with it; it is not possible to be one with a swiftly flowing river. You can never be one with that which has no form, no measure, no quality. It is, that is all." Would you express enlightenment in that way, too, or do you disagree with this statement?

DL: If you are referring to the level of a particular sentient being, a limited being, you could probably say that. But if you are referring to Buddha, there are various interpretations. Even at the stage of enlightenment the mind of Buddha, the clear light mind, is conditioned, momentarily changing. The objects that the mind of Buddha perceives change. Days, weeks, months and so on exist and then cease. As the objects change, so does the mind of the Buddha. Just as objects are endlessly changing, so is the mind of Buddha endlessly changing.

PM: Does this mean that consciousness is endlessly growing or becoming more enlightened?

DL: Buddha's mind always realizes all levels of phenomena. Since all impermanent phenomena are constantly changing, the mind of the Buddha perceiving these changes is, of course, also undergoing change. All created phenomena are in a continual process of change. The mind of Buddha also undergoes this process of change. This kind of change, however, is not a transformative process in the sense of growing, but just in the sense of changing. If you take our mind, however, it is a different matter. It undergoes change not only in the sense of continually perceiving changing situations, but also in the sense of spiritual growth—if we apply the correct methods. In this case, we experience spiritual change along with the passage of time. The culmination of this development is the attainment of Buddhahood, a state in which all positive qualities have been completely acquired and all negative qualities completely eliminated. There is nothing higher to attain, it is the culmination of spiritual development. But the process of change, due to the variety of objects perceived by consciousness, is an endless one, even on the level of Buddhahood. Consciousness is by nature an impermanent, momentary phenomenon.

PM: That was my idea when I asked if a cosmic Buddha existed. In Christianity we have the theory that there was Christ, who incarnated at a certain time in history, but who also develops in universal realms. There is an endless chain of consciousness and also of beings.

DL: There are different aspects of Buddha, called "bodies," or *kayas*.[17] In this connection, the Complete Enjoyment Body, or *Sambhogakaya*, and the Truth Body, or *Dharmakaya*, are explained. From the point of view that the Complete Enjoyment Body can manifest many Emanation Bodies, or *Nirmanakaya*, you could possibly see it as a kind of cosmic Buddha body. But we should not lose sight of the fact that the Complete Enjoyment Body is also an individual.

PM: Is it true that this need not necessarily be an incarnation on the planet earth?

DL: Only the Emanation Body incarnates on earth. The development of consciousness does not necessarily take place only here on earth. But, of course, it must take place within sentient beings. There are sentient beings in various realms—for example, in

---

[17] The three bodies of the Buddha are based on the view that a Buddha is one with the Absolute and manifests in the relative world in order to work for the welfare of all beings. The *Dharmakaya* was initially identified with the teachings given by the historical Buddha Shakyamuni. Only later was it brought together with the other two bodies to form a series. As the true nature of a Buddha, it is timeless, permanent, devoid of characteristics and free from all duality. The *Sambhogakaya* is the result of previous good actions and is realized in enlightenment as a result of a Bodhisattva's accumulated merit. It exhibits the 32 major marks and 80 minor marks of a Buddha and can be perceived only by Bodhisattvas who have attained the last stage of a Bodhisattva's development. The *Nirmanakaya* is embodied in the earthly Buddhas and Bodhisattvas and is projected into the world through the meditation of the Sambhogakaya Buddhas, as a result of their compassion. The task of the Nirmanakaya manifestations is to expound the teachings. Like all human beings, they are subject to the suffering of illness, old age and death, but possess the divine eye and divine hearing.

the heavenly realms. According to Buddhist ideas, there are a number of heavenly realms. Some are within cyclic existence, or *samsara* [18] and others are not.

---

[18] The Sanskrit translation of samsara is "journeying, or cycle of existence." It is the realm in which a being goes through a succession of rebirths in the various modes of existence until it has attained liberation and entered Nirvana. Imprisonment in samsara is conditioned by the three poisons of hatred, desire and ignorance. The type of rebirth in samsara is determined by the karma of the being. Departure from samsara through entry into Nirvana is only possible during a rebirth as a human being. In all other forms of existence, beings cannot end the cyclical process, because they cannot recognize desire and ignorance as the driving forces of samsara and thus overcome them.

An old Tibetan woman

Inauguration of the Norbulingka Temple

The Norbulingka Institute

Buddha Statue in the Main Temple of the Norbulinka Institute

His Holiness the 14th Dalai Lama

His Holiness the 14th Dalai Lama

Dialogue with the His Holiness the 14th Dalai Lama

The Dialogue

56

V.

Individuality and Universality

PM: Regarding universality and individuality, I think that the Buddhist viewpoint is very close to that of Sri Aurobindo,[19] who taught that universal and individual are two companion powers. They are opposite poles of a single manifestation.[20]

DL: In Buddhism, universal consciousness is completely refuted. There is no universal consciousness. Consciousness is always individual. Buddhism does not accept any concept of an all-encompassing consciousness of which our consciousness is a part. It is very important to understand that individuality is on every level, as I have explained. There is nothing cosmic or universal that goes beyond this individual consciousness.

PM: What I mean is that in this individual there can be an expansion into the universal. Lama Anagarika Govinda explains this as follows, *"Individuality and universality are not mutually exclusive values, but two sides of the same reality,*

[19] Aurobindo Ghose (1872-1950) is remembered as one of modern India's most famous sages. Born into a wealthy Bengali family, he was educated in England and became a leading figure in the Bengali nationalist movement. It was during his one-year imprisonment that his spiritual transformation occurred. Upon his release, he renounced the world and published many books on philosophy. Sri Aurobindo described his spiritual approach as "Integral Yoga," which has been hailed as the only new philosophical system to emerge from contemporary India that is firmly rooted in spiritual experience. This yoga purports to offer a viable spiritual path for the present global crises, which Sri Aurobindo understood as a transition from the mental to the supramental consciousness.

[20] Ghose Aurobindo, *The Problem of Rebirth*, Pondicherry, India, 1933, p. 68.

compensating, fulfilling, and complementing each other, and becoming one in the experience of enlightenment. This experience does not dissolve the mind into an amorphous All, but rather brings the realization that the individual itself contains the totality focalized in its very core. Thus, the world that hitherto was experienced as an external reality merges, or is integrated into, the enlightened mind in the moment in which the universality of consciousness is realized. This is the ultimate moment of liberation from the impediments and fetters of ignorance and illusion." [21]

DL: Here we must distinguish between two things. When you refine, develop and strengthen your mental potential, you are not creating a cosmic consciousness that overpowers all other individuals or other consciousnesses. That is not possible. What does happen is that you transform your mind into an omniscient mind. The state of omniscience is sometimes described as the mind pervading all phenomena. This does not mean that the fully developed individual mind now controls all phenomena. Nor does it mean that each individual consciousness comes from this mind. Rather, it means that the mind of an individual is completely enlightened

---

[21] Lama Anagarika Govinda, *Creative Meditation and Multi-Dimensional Consciousness*, Theosopical Publishing House: Wheaton, 1976, p. 48-49.

and, therefore, omniscient. You know everything. There is nothing that your mind cannot know. Pervading all means knowing all in this context.

VI.
Mind and Body

PM: You have stated, *"We Buddhists believe in the existence of a self that moves from life to life and from an ordinary state to the goal of Buddhahood. This self, therefore, is retained. Even a Buddha keeps his self. Buddha Shakyamundi had his own individual identity. This self exists—without beginning, without end. We believe that the individual identity—even that of a Buddha—is retained. This belief is contrary to the Hindu tradition, which postulates Brahman, the universal soul, that unites during moksha, or liberation, with the individual soul, and through which the individual soul loses its identity."* [22]

Could you say how you understand the self in this context?

DL: We have already spoken about that. Here the self refers to sentient beings; in other words, a person, who is designated by the five psychophysical aggregates, and not by the independent or absolute self, in the sense of atman, which Buddhists refute.

For example, there can be no argument that there are six human beings here in this room. It is a fact that there are six people in this room. That is reality and not an illusion. On that basis we can develop love and compassion, or negative feelings toward

[22] Discussion between H.H. the Dalai Lama and Mr. Troemel, President of Adyar Verlag, Germany

one another. Whether we develop negative or positive feelings, these are directed toward the person, not their body or mind. When we speak about the action of killing a human being, to whom are we referring? We condemn the act of taking human life. Although the human being, or person, is not something we can pinpoint directly, human beings are an accepted convention. On the basis of this conventionally accepted existence, we reject the notion of killing a human being.

Let us examine what the actual object is when we talk about human beings. Is it the human body? The answer is no. In order to save the life of a person, it may even be necessary to remove a part or parts of the body. Maybe an arm or leg has to be amputated to save that person's life. Removing the head would probably mean the death of that person! But other parts of the body can be removed as a means to saving that person's life. Let us look at the mind. Sometimes it is hyperactive, alert and so sophisticated that the person becomes unhappy. For this reason medication may be appropriate to reduce the alertness of that person's mind. This would improve his sense of well-being. This shows that the mind is a human mind, but not the human being itself. In the same way, the body is that of a human being but is not the human being itself. Body and mind are the basis of the human being, but not the human being itself. So, when we analyze, we cannot find the human being, cannot identify it concretely.

Even some modern physicists say that, from the point of view of quantum physics, there is no reality. That means when we go very deep and try to pinpoint a certain phenomenon, we will never be able to find it. At least that goes for the material world. It does not go for consciousness, which is not the object of their analysis.

PM: David Bohm [23] says that even elementary particles have consciousness.

DL: That is difficult to say. What is the meaning of consciousness? That is rather complicated. I think there are forms of subtle energy that cannot necessarily be called consciousness. There is subtle energy that is related to consciousness. But there is also subtle energy that is without consciousness. My point is this: outside of this body and mind, we cannot identify this self or human being. Yet we have to accept that there is a human being. When we investigate, we cannot find what the actual human being is. When we do not investigate, the hu-

---

[23] The physicist David Bohm was a pupil of Albert Einstein and one of the main partners in dialogues with Jiddu Krishnamurti. Without doubt, he can be regarded as one of the most foreseeing scientists of our century. His philosophical interpretations of quantum theory reveal fascinating dimensions of a new world view. He died in 1992.

man being obviously exists. The conclusion is that the human being, in other words the human self, exists as a designation of its psychophysical aggregates. It is this conventional self that has been going from life to life since beginningless time.

VII.
Buddhist Meditation

PM: My last question is a practical one. In the *Essence of Refined Gold,*[24] and also in one of your meetings with Professor Carl-Friedrich von Weizsäcker in Germany, you spoke much more about the esoteric teachings in Buddhism than ever before. You mentioned, for example, that the stories about the Tibetan master Milarepa[25] were true, and that he had used his extraordinary faculties, such as the ability to fly. Then you added, *"These are not fairy tales."* It seems that there is much deep esoteric knowledge in Buddhism that the West does not know, but that could be used for our own transformation. What can people in the West do? What

---

[24] The 3rd Dalai Lama, *Essence of Refined Gold*, Snow Lion Publications: Ithaca, New York, 1985. The 14th Dalai Lama wrote a commentary on this text written by the 3rd Dalai Lama (1543-1588). It is itself a direct commentary on the concise version of the work *"The Graduated Path of Spiritual Practice,"* written by the great Tibetan saint, Tsongkhapa (1357-1419).

[25] A famous 11th century Tibetan saint. His name in Tibetan is translated as "Mila who wears the cotton cloth of an ascetic." After trials of the utmost difficulty imposed on him by his teacher Marpa, Milarepa received complete teachings from him. His diligent and exemplary exertion in the realization of these teachings resulted in the founding of the Kagyupa school. When Milarepa was seven, his father died and the family property fell into the hands of greedy relatives, who treated him and his mother very badly. To avenge these injuries, he learned to master the destructive forces of nature and killed many people with a fierce storm. Wishing to atone for his deed, Milarepa turned to a teacher who later sent him to Marpa. For six years, he served as Marpa's servant. During this period, Marpa subjected him to extraordinarily harsh training, which brought him to such despair that he was near suicide. After Milarepa's evil deeds had been purified in this fashion, Marpa began preparing him for a life of solitude. Milarepa lived for many years in complete seclusion in icy mountain caves, devoting himself to meditation practice. After nine years of uninterrupted solitude, Milarepa accepted students and began to teach people with his songs.

71

could Your Holiness, or Buddhists, do to bring that knowledge to the Western world?

DL: That is not a simple matter, as it requires a large number of practices on different levels. When we talk about subtle levels of body and mind, these cannot be attained through one meditation alone. I do think, however, that certain preliminaries can be practiced by ordinary people, or can be carried out for experimental purposes. They can be adopted for one's mental health, as yoga exercises are done for one's physical health. But you should be aware that these practices are a part of the Buddhist system and can only lead to deeper experiences when understood and carried out in that context. The realization of *shunyata*, or emptiness, and the training of *Bodhicitta*, or altruism, are indispensable if you want proper results. Without these it is really questionable whether the meditations would be effective.

PM: Does that mean the esoteric teachings cannot be practiced easily in the Western world?

DL: It has nothing to do with the West or the East. The point is that you need practices that are systematic and complete in order to achieve the desired results.

PM: Is there no Buddhist way of leading a normal worldly life in the West? Do we have to come to Dharamsala and study seriously under the lifelong guidance of a Buddhist master?

DL: I don't know. As I mentioned, it is indeed possible to do preliminary practices. How you develop after that is a matter of what you study and how you implement it. I think that certain results can be attained without having to do deeper practices. That is, they can also be done by non-Buddhists. For example, it is possible for one to achieve separation of the subtle and gross levels of the body, or to achieve some clarity of mind and control the breath for a few hours.

VIII.
Talk in Salzburg

PM: May I start with a very personal question. If you look back through time, through your very unusual incarnation, what do you think was the deepest experience of love you've had in this life? What was the experience that moved you most?

DL: I can't remember just one single incident. There are two main forms of moving experiences. I am very affected when I see needy, suffering people and poor, suffering animals, or insects. A deep feeling of emotional concern, or compassion, emerges. I am also deeply touched emotionally when I meditate, especially during analytical meditations on compassion or similar topics, or when I give a Buddhist teaching on the value and necessity of compassion and similar qualities. On many occasions I have wept during public teachings.

PM: Does this happen when people come to you for advice and guidance in their lives, and when you sense that you can help them on their path? Are these the situations that create this kind of emotion?

DL: These deep emotions emerge when I observe suffering, or when I think about the value of compassion. There were occasions when I met with Tibetans who had escaped from Tibet and who had suffered a great deal. Because they trusted me and expected too much from me, with the compassion there was also a desperate feeling that I could not do much to help them. Knowing that they expected me to solve all their problems increased my responsibility and at the same time imposed a limitation. The result was a combination of sincere compassion and desperatation. So, sometimes, I just feel sad.

PM: I understand. One of the statements I like most is when you said, *"A sad human being cannot influence reality. If you are sad or depressed, you cannot influence reality."* You once said that.

DL: That's right. It won't help to solve the problem. In other words, from a deeper perspective, all human beings are brothers and sisters. When you face a so-called enemy, that enemy only exists on a relative level. Then, if you harbor hatred or ill-feeling toward that person, the feeling itself does not hurt the enemy. It only harms your own peace of mind, and eventually your own health. This is what I usually say. And, also, too much worry will not help to eliminate a problem. It only harms your own peace of mind. The worse part is that such states of mind destroy the best part of your brain, and impede your ability to judge the situation. When your mind is depressed or agitated, it becomes more difficult to solve a problem.

PM: What is your advice for the many people, especially in the West, who suffer from depression? Doctors and therapists often find it difficult to treat people with depression. Perhaps they do not have a practical therapy for the future.

DL: On the level of just being a human being, not as a Buddhist, not as a religious believer, I usually tell people I believe that human nature is positive. The basic human nature is something pure. From birth, we possess the potential for all good qualities. Knowing that we have the ability to realize that potential is the basis of self confidence. When someone's mental state is agitated, that person usually only looks at the negative side and does not take a broader perspective. No matter how tragic an incident might be, it still has some positive aspects. Everything is relative. One should, therefore, try to look at the situation from a different viewpoint. Another way to view difficult situations is to understand that many other human beings also have the same problem. This person is not a unique case. I think depressed people have the feeling that they are the only unfortunate people and that their situation is hopeless. But other people face even greater problems. That is another way to relieve mental depression. That is usually my advice.

PM: I would like to ask another question. It is about some information I came across when I wrote a biography of Krishnamurti. You met him in 1956.

DL: Yes, I met him a few times.

PM: … and you planned to meet him again in 1985 …

DL: True!

PM: But, unfortunately, at the time of the planned meeting, Indira Gandhi was murdered. I found in Krishnamurti's papers that he wanted to discuss the question of religious tradition, and especially religious rituals, with you. What is your view on Krishnamurti's criticism of all kinds of religious traditions?

DL: (laughing) I don't know! Sometimes his approach, his way of thinking, was on the negative side. One of his close friends at one time expressed to me that she was very fond of Krishnamurti. We had a discussion on ultimate reality—*shunyata* or emptiness—according to the Buddhist perspective, especially Nagarjuna's [26] explanation that the meaning of emptiness is just a negation. But this emptiness

<hr>

[26] Nagarjuna is one of the most important philosophers in Buddhism and the founder of the Madhyamika school. Although there are no reliable dates for his life, it is believed he lived in India during the 2nd or 3rd century. Nagarjuna's major accom-

means the emptiness of independent existence, the relative nature, that things are interdependent. Because their nature is interdependent, their nature is the absence of independent existence. So voidness, or emptiness, does not mean just nothingness. Nagarjuna emphasizes both sides. Interdependence is a positive phenomenon and emptiness is a negative phenomenon. My guest then said that, when she heard Krishnamurti's explanation, it appeared that there is only emptiness. But, according to His Holiness' explanation, ultimate reality is not only nothingness, but there is something positive as well. I don't mean Krishnamurti's philosophy in particular but, through the centuries, certain schools of philosophy were primarily critical and negating. If your mind meditates on nothingness as reality, or remains only in it, it may give rise to hopelessness. I think this type of philosophy does not help very much. There are other types of philosophy that do not explain ultimate reality as an emptiness but stress that, on the relative or conventional level, everything is possible

---

plishment was his systematization and deeping of the teaching presented in the Prajnaparamita, or Perfection of Wisdom, sutra. He developed a special dialectic based on a reductio ad absurdum of opponents' positions. Starting from the premise that each thing exists only in relation to its opposite, he showed that all things are only relative and without essence. They are empty (shunya). Nagarjuna's methodological approach of rejecting all opposites is the basis for the Middle Way of the Madhyamikas and is directly connected with the teaching of the Buddha. This middle position is clearly expressed in the eight negations — no elimination, no production, no destruction, no eternity, no unity, no manifoldness, no arriving and no departing.

and exists. This type of philosophy is more well-balanced. It's approach seems more complete.

PM: I think Krishnamurti would agree with you in your definition of shunyata, or emptiness. His criticism was that the approach to traditional religion would only lead you to some kind of false image of what he called truth. As a result, his idea was to eliminate all kinds of traditions. My observation in the biography I wrote about him was that he cut off too much. He spoke from a level of high realization, while ordinary human beings are not at that level. Krishnamurti had no way to connect these two levels.

DL: I am a Buddhist and I'm sorry I may rely too much on the Buddha's teachings. Of course, I also have the liberty to investigate even what Buddha said, because the basic Buddhist attitude, particularly the Mahayana Buddhist attitude, is that you should rely on investigation and experiment rather than on words, even if it's the word of the Buddha. If you find a contradiction in your own experience, you have the liberty to deny that this is the Buddha's word. However, I greatly admire, respect and prefer Nagarjuna's approach. I think in order to realize the deeper reality, the deeper nature, Nagarjuna and his followers (like Candrakirti's [27]) way of reasoning and way of investigation is very, very useful. So, I adopted these methods. If I reject these methods, and say that there is something wrong in all these great teachers and masters' experience, that means I am saying I'm better and more progressed than even these masters. That is very difficult to say. I think these great masters of the past were also very, very sharp-minded.

PM: In a discussion you had with Prof. Renée Webber, [28] you made an interesting statement about the self. You stated, *"There is a mere I, or a mere self, of which you can say 'my former lifetime, my future lifetime.' The mere I, or the mere self, existed in the former lifetime, exists in this lifetime, and will exist in the next lifetime. Yesterday's I, today's I and tomorrow's I are, in a sense, the same I. But, in another sense, yesterday's I is no more, it is really gone, and tomorrow's I is yet to come. As a whole, the continuum of the I moment-by-moment extends through the whole process."* My question is based on your approach to the self, which is a little bit different from what I understood about Buddhism. If the deepest meaning of life is to realize happi-

---

[27] Candrakirti is famous for his lucid and profound commentary on the work of Nagarjuna and Aryadeva, who dominated the beginning of the Madhyamika school. He lived in India at the end of the 6th century and in the early part of the 7th century. Chandrakirti made an essential commentary on the Karikas by Nagarjuna in his work Prasannapada (Clear Words), which tried to restore the Madhyamika doctrine to its original purity. He also distinguished himself in the field of logic, which advanced the development of Nagarjuna and Aryadeva's thought.

[28] Renée Webber, *Dialogues with Scientists and Sages*, Arkana: London, 1990

ness or bliss, then there must be someone or something that experiences this bliss.

DL: Yes, that is the I!

PM: But how can this be compatible with the philosophy of the non-self, the non-atman?

DL: There is no problem. The philosophy of non-self does not deny the existence of the I. The theory of non-self was developed primarily to address non-Buddhist philosophies. Their concept is that besides this body and mind, some kind of owner of this body and mind can be identified. That is called "atma." That atma is said to be permanent. They also use this reason to support the assertion that, if there was not such an atma besides the body and mind, there would be no possibility of accepting the concept of rebirth. That is their concept. Their difficulty in upholding this view is based on the problem they have in accepting a mere I.

Now, from the Buddhist viewpoint, for example, we can say there are five persons in this room, four male and one female. When we speak of a person, this includes both male and female. But, if we just say "person," we cannot identify it as male or female. This is the difficulty of explaining the existence of the general and the specific. There may be a lot of argument, but we accept that there is a mere person, mere people. There is a general category of "person," and all five people belong to this category. We can only determine whether or not someone is a person, based on that particular person. We can communicate, we can understand. But if we investigate what exactly is that person, we cannot find it. That is the concept of mere I.

In the case of a particular person, besides this body and mind, we cannot identify anything else as an I, or as a self. The self is just mere designation based on the combination of body and mind. Because it is just simply designated, there is no independent I, or self, apart from this body and mind. The Buddhist's conclusion is that the I, or the concept of I, is just a mere I, designated by the combination of the five skandhas.[29] In other words, body and mind.

However, body and mind is not necessarily the obvious body and mind alone. There are more subtle levels of the body and mind. Therefore, even if this solid body and gross level of mind dissolve, the subtle body and subtle mind are still there. So, the basis of mere I is still there. Without distinguishing the solid body from the subtle body, we can say that there is always a continuation of body and mind. That is the basis of the mere I,

---

[29] The Sanskrit word skandha is translated as "group, aggregate or heap." It is the term used for the five aggregates, which are corporeality or form, sensation, perception, mental formations and consciousness. The characteristics of the skandhas are birth, old age, death, duration and change. They are regarded as without essence (anatman), impermanent (anitya), empty (shunya) and suffering-ridden (duhkha).

which exists from beginningless time. Sometimes, due to that subtle body and subtle mind, a solid body and a grosser level of mind, such as ours, develop.

PM: If it is beginningless, is it also endless?

DL: From the Mahayana Buddhist viewpoint it is also endless. According to the Theravada system, when someone reaches Buddhahood, there is no more continuation of an I after the physical or gross body passes away. That is the theory of the Vaibhashika school. A faction of the Chittamatra school and the Madhyamika schools of thought both accept the continuation of mind, even after Nirvana.[30] Their point is that the subtle mind, the ultimate nature of mind, is pure. Because the basic nature of mind is neutral, or pure, there is no reason to believe that the mind disappears if all the negativities have been purified or removed. As a result, mind as well as matter will remain. It is beginningless, it has no end.

Now let's address the concept of I. In my own case, for example, I can say that I am a Buddhist monk. But, when I was four years old, I could not

---

[30] Nirvana is translated in Sanskrit as 'extinction'. In the understanding of early Buddhism, Nirvana is departure from the cycle of rebirths and entry into an entirely different mode of existence. It requires a complete overcoming of the three poisons - desire, hatred and delusion - and the cessation of active volition. It means freedom from the effects of karma. Nirvana is unconditioned. Its qualities are the absence of arising, subsisting, changing and passing away. The Mahayana concept of Nirvana is conceived as oneness with the absolute or the unity of samsara and

have said that I was a Buddhist monk. Also, I am Tibetan. That I has existed since my birth. That I was there. But the I which is a monk had not yet developed. At the age of seven, I took the monk vow. From that time the I which is a monk began. Now I am a refugee. That refugee I has existed only since 1959. So the I which is a human being is a bigger one. The I from my previous life is a still bigger I. The I of this life is shorter. And in this life the refugee I is even shorter. With this example, you can see that one single basis has many designations. They are all Tibetan, but nominally different, since there are different aspects of one entity.

Since we accept the concept of a mere thing, the I that exists is an imputation. Imputation is how these things can be possible. If we need some kind of solid basis, there should be three I's. For example, the I that exists from birth (the Tibetan I), then another I that exists since I became a monk, then another I that exists since I became a refugee. So today there should be three I's. But, in reality, this is not the case, there is just one I. But, at the same time, that one I can have many different aspects. I can, therefore, say that we can accept the refugee I and monk I and the Tibetan I.

Here is the difference. It is said that words and thought are eliminative engagers, whereas direct per-

transcendence. It is also described as dwelling in the experience of the absolute bliss in perceiving one's identity with the Absolute and as freedom from attachment to illusions, affects and desires.

ception is a holistic engager. There is a difference between the act of the sense organs and the act of conceptual thought. When I look at a flower, although my mental consciousness does not necessarily recognize it, the eye consciousness is actually seeing the color, shape and the nature of momentary change. All this is seen by the sense perception organs. Whatever aspects are there, are experienced. The object as a whole is seen. But it is not necessarily identified by thought. The act of conceptual thought is different. When I have a thought about color, for example, thought perceives just one aspect of the flower, although there are many more aspects, such as the variety of colors, the shape, the smell, the momentary changing and so forth. The same is true for the word "color." It only identifies one thing, not the whole quality. Whereas eye consciousness sees the whole object. The conceptual thought just picks up one aspect and eliminates or blocks all other aspects. It is, therefore, called an eliminative engager. It apprehends one aspect by eliminating all others.

In the same way, the I has many aspects. But when we use the word, or concept, I, we refer to only one aspect.

Thank you very much.

PM: Thank you, and all the best to you and your people.